Sometimes, life's challenges seem so overwhelming it is hard to feel optimistic about the future. You may feel that failures outweigh successes, or there seems to be a more considerable loss for every win. I remember many days when I was frustrated and overwhelmed because I had the perfect plan and worked to execute it, only to encounter an unplanned obstacle for which I seemed to have no solution. Despite words of solace and spiritual encouragement, I was only soothed for a short period. It is in moments where I feel the most distressed that I have to find something to ground me and help to de-escalate my feelings of anxiety and frustration.

I recall one evening when I was standing in my dining room. The ceiling had been gutted after a waterline burst, and the water damage had spread from my dining room to my living room walls and floor. The insurance check seemed too small to cover the massive damages. I had cried at least three times, shaking my fist toward God, asking why I could not seem to find a moment of peace. Yet, that morning, the moment of peace found me, and all I could do was be thankful that I had a roof over my head to protect my son and me from the rain and cold weather. Standing in the middle of my dining room with the beams of my ceiling exposed,

Introduction

I closed my eyes and listened to the peacefulness of the rain. I thanked God for the resources that would help improve my home's condition. I thanked God that the damages were fixable. Then, I continued to build my list of things for which I needed to be thankful. I realized that despite the capacity of the challenge I was facing, I was enormously blessed. However, I had been so overwhelmed by my present situation that I had lost sight of the big picture. I needed a moment to decompress, reflect, and remember that I had many reasons to be thankful.

That is precisely what this journal is about-reflecting and thankfulness. During those moments when everything around you seems chaotic and you are worried about the future, take time to look back. Look at where you've been, where you are, what you've gained, and what you've accomplished. You have so much to be thankful for. Sometimes, the answers you need come from the experiences that have shaped your life. Thankfulness is not just a one-time or one-moment experience; it's part of a lifestyle. An attitude of gratitude can bring more good things into your life, shift your mood, and elevate your future.

Introduction

So, for the next thirty days, commit yourself to taking thirty minutes a day to reflect and write about it. Use your writings to center yourself and release frustration, fear, and sadness. Allow your pen to help you celebrate the past and write away the fears and worries of the future.

One day of Thankfulness   date: _____

_____
_____
_____
_____
_____
_____
_____
_____
_____
_____
_____
_____
_____
_____
_____
_____
_____
_____
_____

Celebrate where you are; anticipate where you will go.

Celebrate where you are; anticipate where you will go.

Two days of thankfulness   date: _____

_____
_____
_____
_____
_____
_____
_____
_____
_____
_____
_____
_____
_____
_____
_____
_____
_____
_____

Every day may not be perfect, but there's a perfect plan for you.

Every day may not be perfect, but there's a perfect plan for you.

Three days of Thankfulness

date: _____

_____
_____
_____
_____
_____
_____
_____
_____
_____
_____
_____
_____
_____
_____
_____
_____
_____
_____
_____
_____

Taking care of your health is a reflection of gratitude.

Taking care of your health is a reflection of gratitude.

Four days of thankfulness

_____

_____

_____

_____

_____

_____

_____

_____

_____

_____

_____

_____

_____

_____

_____

_____

_____

_____

_____

Follow your dreams, and don't give up!

Follow your dreams, and don't give up!

Five days of thankfulness

date: _____

_____

_____

_____

_____

_____

_____

_____

_____

_____

_____

_____

_____

_____

_____

_____

_____

_____

_____

_____

_____

Be gentle with yourself; you are doing your best!

Be gentle with yourself; you are doing your best!

Six days of Thankfulness   date: _____

_____
_____
_____
_____
_____
_____
_____
_____
_____
_____
_____
_____
_____
_____
_____
_____
_____
_____
_____

That experience didn't break you. It made you stronger!

That experience didn't break you. It made you stronger!

Seven days of Thankfulness

date: _____

_____
_____
_____
_____
_____
_____
_____
_____
_____
_____
_____
_____
_____
_____
_____
_____
_____
_____
_____
_____
_____

Sometimes, the silver lining is that you survived!

Sometimes, the silver lining is that you survived!

Eight days of thankfulness

date: _____

_____
_____
_____
_____
_____
_____
_____
_____
_____
_____
_____
_____
_____
_____
_____
_____
_____
_____

Your journey is inspiration to someone else.

Your journey is inspiration to someone else.

Nine days of Thankfulness

date: _____

_____
_____
_____
_____
_____
_____
_____
_____
_____
_____
_____
_____
_____
_____
_____
_____
_____
_____

Excellence is a result of not giving up!

Excellence is a result of not giving up!

Ten days of Thankfulness

date: _____

_____

_____

_____

_____

_____

_____

_____

_____

_____

_____

_____

_____

_____

_____

_____

_____

_____

_____

_____

_____

Love yourself just as much as you love everyone else.

Love yourself just as much as you love everyone else.

Eleven days of thankfulness

date: _____

_____
_____
_____
_____
_____
_____
_____
_____
_____
_____
_____
_____
_____
_____
_____
_____
_____
_____
_____
_____
_____

An attitude of gratitude can change your day.

An attitude of gratitude can change your day.

Twelve days of thankfulness

date: _____

_____

_____

_____

_____

_____

_____

_____

_____

_____

_____

_____

_____

_____

_____

_____

_____

_____

_____

Be thankful for the small things; they make a big difference.

Be thankful for the small things; they make a big
difference.

Thirteen days of thankfulness

date: _____

Setbacks don't ruin you; they shape you.

Setbacks don't ruin you; they shape you.

Fourteen days of thankfulness

date: _____

_____
_____
_____
_____
_____
_____
_____
_____
_____
_____
_____
_____
_____
_____
_____
_____
_____
_____

Appreciation leads to elevation!

Appreciation leads to elevation!

Fifteen days of Thankfulness

date: _____

_____

_____

_____

_____

_____

_____

_____

_____

_____

_____

_____

_____

_____

_____

_____

_____

_____

_____

_____

_____

_____

Honor those before you by doing your best each day.

Honor those before you by doing your best each day.

Sixteen days of thankfulness

date: _____

_____

_____

_____

_____

_____

_____

_____

_____

_____

_____

_____

_____

_____

_____

_____

_____

_____

_____

Gratitude is honoring those who supported you.

_____

_____

_____

_____

_____

_____

_____

_____

_____

_____

_____

_____

_____

_____

_____

_____

_____

Gratitude is honoring those who supported you.

Seventeen days of Thankfulness   date: _____

_____
_____
_____
_____
_____
_____
_____
_____
_____
_____
_____
_____
_____
_____
_____
_____
_____
_____
_____
_____
_____

Appreciation yields commendation!

Appreciation yields commendation!

Eighteen days of thankfulness   date: _____

_____
_____
_____
_____
_____
_____
_____
_____
_____
_____
_____
_____
_____
_____
_____
_____
_____
_____
_____

Philanthropy and gratitude are powerful partnerships!

Philanthropy and gratitude are powerful partnerships!

Nineteen days of thankfulness   date: _____

_____
_____
_____
_____
_____
_____
_____
_____
_____
_____
_____
_____
_____
_____
_____
_____
_____
_____
_____
_____
_____
_____

A positive attitude is good for physical and emotional health.

A positive attitude is good for physical and emotional health.

Twenty days of Thankfulness   date: _____

_____
_____
_____
_____
_____
_____
_____
_____
_____
_____
_____
_____
_____
_____
_____
_____
_____
_____
_____

Let us give the same grace we hope to receive.

Let us give the same grace we hope to receive.

Twenty-One days of Thankfulness   date: _____

_____
_____
_____
_____
_____
_____
_____
_____
_____
_____
_____
_____
_____
_____
_____
_____
_____
_____
_____
_____
_____
_____

May ou bring light & joy to every room you enter.

May ou bring light & joy to every room you enter.

Twenty-Two days of thankfulness   date: _____

_____

_____

_____

_____

_____

_____

_____

_____

_____

_____

_____

_____

_____

_____

_____

_____

_____

_____

_____

_____

Find delight in moments of quietness.

Find delight in moments of quietness.

Twenty-Three days of Thankfulness   date: _____

_____
_____
_____
_____
_____
_____
_____
_____
_____
_____
_____
_____
_____
_____
_____
_____
_____
_____
_____
_____

Thankful people have boundaries, too.

Thankful people have boundaries, too.

Twenty-four days of thankfulness   date: _____

_____
_____
_____
_____
_____
_____
_____
_____
_____
_____
_____
_____
_____
_____
_____
_____
_____
_____
_____

Kindness is not an obligation, but it is a necessity.

Kindness is not an obligation, but it is a necessity.

Twenty-five days of thankfulness   date: _____

Gratitude is reflected in the seeds you sow.

Gratitude is reflected in the seeds you sow.

Twenty-six days of thankfulness   date: _____

_____
_____
_____
_____
_____
_____
_____
_____
_____
_____
_____
_____
_____
_____
_____
_____
_____
_____
_____
_____

Welcome change with an open heart. It may lead to
many blessings.

Welcome change with an open heart. It may lead to many blessings.

Twenty-seven days of thankfulness   date: _____

_____

_____

_____

_____

_____

_____

_____

_____

_____

_____

_____

_____

_____

_____

_____

_____

_____

_____

_____

_____

Reflect on the past. Appreciate the present. Anticipate the future.

_____

_____

_____

_____

_____

_____

_____

_____

_____

_____

_____

_____

_____

_____

_____

_____

_____

_____

Reflect on the past. Appreciate the present. Anticipate the future.

Twenty-eight days of thankfulness   date: _____

_____
_____
_____
_____
_____
_____
_____
_____
_____
_____
_____
_____
_____
_____
_____
_____
_____
_____
_____
_____
_____
_____
_____

Align yourself spiritually and emotionally to create a peaceful lifestyle.

Align yourself spiritually and emotionally to create a peaceful lifestyle.

Twenty-nine days of thankfulness   date: _____

_____
_____
_____
_____
_____
_____
_____
_____
_____
_____
_____
_____
_____
_____
_____
_____
_____
_____
_____
_____

Keep writing. You have so much to be thankful for!

Keep writing. You have so much to be thankful for!

Thirty days of thankfulness

date: _____

_____
_____
_____
_____
_____
_____
_____
_____
_____
_____
_____
_____
_____
_____
_____
_____
_____
_____
_____
_____

Live each day with a spirit of gratitude!

Live each day with a spirit of gratitude!

Made in the USA
Columbia, SC
31 January 2024

31212819R00035